JOANSTOWN
AND OTHER POEMS

MICHAEL GILKES

JOANSTOWN
AND OTHER POEMS.

P E E P A L   T R E E

First published in Great Britain in 2002
Peepal Tree Press Ltd
17 King's Avenue
Leeds LS6 1QS

ISBN 1-900715-76-7

CONTENTS

PROLOGUE

Noon on the barbecue of this beach. Sun striking
the dimpled gong of the sea. My daughter, diving.
Adjusting the aperture of my fish-eye lens I watch her
surfacing, dolphin-head pouring with hair, wearing
a clownish dolphin-smile, fins propelling her in
a dolphin-swim, backwards, yelling "Watch me, Dad!
I'll do a back-flip."
[flashback: Dolphin Government School. Zoom to close-up.
The school bell. Focus on one small boy
reading. Background of boys, bookbags, bicycles.
Narrator: "Books were rivers he could slip into
and breathe. [Dissolve to illustration from *The Water Babies*]
With ease he could feel, in a Shakespeare lyric: 'when icicles
hang by the wall...' the chill of a wood in winter,
or swing with Tarzan's apes through the tall canopy
of trees.
[archival film: Brickdam, Georgetown in the mid-forties]
At Queen's College he was leisurely, lazy,
Indifferent to failure or success.
Elected Clown Prince of Misrule, a quasi-
Quasimodo humped over a wooden desk,
fool, cutting her name into the wood,
oblivious, stubborn back bent to the task
like Esmeralda's goat, subverting Good
with rank innocence, wearing a fool's mask
to disarm the cruel boyhood rule of strength.

Sanctuary was that silent water-world
of books. Searching for depth he swam the length
and breadth of secondary school, tested
the rivers, creeks, the mud-brown sea, the Wireless pool

looking for anchor; some deep, harbouring bay.
[slow pan: the sea between the roundhouse and Groyne beach]
One day she stepped into the sea as he
was leaving. In that crossing, without speech,
he knew that she would be that bay.
[the Barrack street house, the seawall esplanade]
Each Sunday, riding past that crowded gallery
of faces, he hoped his faith would find her there,
hands clasped upon her lap, demurely, back
upright as her piano, head a halo
of blown hair, the lovely face turned sideways, so,
averted with an absolutely natural grace;
the smile gentle, but still dimpling her cheek.
He prayed that such authentic gold would stay.
Those steady hazel eyes, Pacific-deep,
embracing silence, could say all there was to say.
It would be years before he saw them weep
for what the fool had thrown away..."

That brown head bobbing turned out to be
a gutted coconut buoyed by the sea.
Sun now silvering the blue. My dolphin-daughter,
beached, flops dripping on the sand, her golden
skin reflecting the sun's gold. A welter
of small sea-creatures clings to her hair.
I stare as my webbed fingers grow into branches,
my trunk an old, humped sea-almond tree,
its rust-caked, heart-shaped leaves a shade, a shelter...

JOANSTOWN

1. The town

Girl and town are interwoven by those magic years:
try to conjure one the other one appears.
Think of something elegant, handsome, hand-sewn:
the clothes she wore with such stylish simplicity.
She made them from patterns she saw in town. The town
was appliquéd : silk-cotton and samaan, the rough embroidery
of their roots adding a creole hemstitch to the strict
colonial cross-hatching of avenues, bridges, canals,
the roads straight-stitched, rain-sprinkled, steam-ironed
by hissing tyres.
Main street split and ran, like children out of school,
on both sides of that leaf-patterned, flower-printed avenue
to the slate-grey, granite hem of the final sea wall.
Entering High Street you entered a Hobbema avenue:
overhead an arch of green and then an arch of blue.
The town was a Dutch linen tablecloth hand-crafted with care
for setting out a city's treasured silverware.
Place St. George's cathedral on its centrepiece, there.
Next, the castle-shaped iced-wedding-cake Town Hall
with its roccoco tower. Now lower the stained glass rotunda
on to its wooden gallery and set down the Park Hotel.
The Assembly Rooms. Good. The Hand-in-Hand Mutual,
its iron filigree patterns plundered from the city's fretworked
treasury of wood. (The treachery of wood!
Those curlicues would be repeated in the flames
that curled like leaves the zinc roofs of Joanstown).
Ease down the Public Buildings on its tiered, tired
Greco-Roman arches, pseudo-marble columns
and bald-pated dome, dim echo of patrician Rome.
The Victoria Law Courts, half-timbered, Tudor style,

a chessboard where, alone, the white queen reigns:
Victoria, plinthed, testing the weight of a breadfruit-sized globe
in one royal palm, the coiled folds of her robe
recalling the capsized Victoria Regia's monstrous varicose veins.

If life was stayed and stockinged, stubbornly Victorian,
at least it was Victrola simple, a record he'd put on
while aunt Aria pedalled her sewing machine upstairs,
the Singer staccato-humming its own dialect song
in harmony with His Master's Voice, both needles knitting
girl and town, their voices double-stitched in unison.
The gift of double vision was Joanstown's bequest.
Everything he saw was cursed and blessed.
The lighthouse beam patrolled our evening skies :
A Lighthouse match hissed once and snakes of flame had entered
Paradise.

2. The Lighthouse

Before it shrank into the logo for Lighthouse matches
and then went out, a blackened stick, it was something to see.
Sun glinted on its bright encircling brass, a small
version of the seawall bandstand elevated, held
up by a concrete red-and-white-striped column, like a tall
bandsman in uniform topped by his tuba's shining bell.

There was a British fortress on that Dutch seawall:
brown surf, brown sand, brown sea habitual as the whiskey
Captain Henwood downed, licking his Errol Flynn moustache.
Horseguards inspection at four, roundhouse cannon at six
firing the street lamps first in Fort Street, Barrack Street,
and then, when Main Street caught, igniting the town. They built
the lighthouse to warn of mud banks and just for fun,
refashioning in English what the Dutch had done.
The thing looked like a stick of Brighton rock candy,
O.H.M.S. ER II stamped on the top
and running (I guessed) all the way through.
Decked with Christmas lights it was a pierside dandy, pissed,
a swaggering Pearly King, nostalgic pink and white reminder
of the seaside towns and fish-and-chips shops they missed.
By day it stood sober, imperially red and white
against the blue, the lighting cue for sunsets to come on,
its strict, right-wheeling lamp impartial as the match
whose methylated-blue green flash once set the town alight.

The spill from its beam catches the leaning torso of a girl
who begins to glow in the lamp of a Demerara window
at the top of a tall house. A boy on a bicycle is leaving
the darkness under the house. She waves as he rides away:
dark, light-light, then dark, the lighthouse semaphore.

He thinks of that rusting flagship, the Key Holt,
once Sandhurst-shine, marooned far out from shore
and waves, straight-armed, hand cocked like a man firing a flare,
looking back until the window goes dark and the glare
of the lighthouse beam is left stroking the space where her light had been.
He will not sleep tonight, thinking of lighthouse beams.
She will sleep thinking of him.
He will find her entering his dreams.

3. Thirty-three Barrack Street, Kingston

Miss Winifred McDavid was well known
to be the country's finest piano teacher
and stern guardian of the lovely Joan.
None of the other schools could ever reach her
standard: lessons there would be a dream come true.
There was a vacancy! His father shook his head :
"No. Your brother should go. He's older. You
will go next time." His dream fell dead.
A letter would be sent confirming what was said.
He'd take the letter. With luck it might give him
another chance to see those hazel eyes
turning again to look at him with mild surprise.

A sudden downpour as he turned into her street,
rain falling hard out of a clear blue sky.
If he took shelter underneath her house
and had the luck to meet her there, how could he speak
to her, weak with the love that he was ravished by?
Wet with his shame, he rode into a salt-goods shop
already filling up with cowards sheltering.
He was in hell. Heaven was across the street
curtained by rain. He could hear her playing arpeggios.
(that would be his brother's bliss, not his, not his)
All he could do was curse his luck and wait.
Caught in that hell-mouth, he was already too late.
The envelope he carried had sealed his fate.

The rain stopped. He wheeled his cycle out.
Hell-mouth emptied its dark shelterers
with their damp bags and bundles out onto the street.
On the other side she'd come out and was sitting astride

her bike on the bridge outside her gate. He forgot
what he'd come to do. She was Nike tying her
shoelaces, supple back bent to the task.
Her blue-green uniform, belted at the waist,
showed the shy swell of her breasts, brown
ringlets of hair escaping the brown rim
of her straw hat with its embroidered Bishop's High School
band. Those grey-green eyes had turned to him
and caught his look. He saw her blush and turn away
and every fibre in his body shook.

Forgive his lovesick adoration of
that girl riding to school, brown arms bare,
sapodilla-warm, her hat a Gaugin halo,
the afternoon rain-sprinkled and sun-kissed like Debussy's
l'aprés midi d'une faune, bright drops falling from
the immortelles like diamonds, like the scales that fell
from her piano. He would ride out of his way
to take the road she took to ride to school
hoping to meet her, tongue-tied when he did.
Sick with cowardice the fool would ride under
her house to hear her play, then ride away.
It was his Mecca now, thirty-three Barrack
Street. It had become the image of his love:
darkness below, a world of music above.

He would become a showman, make tigers purr,
elephants kneel down on rubber knees.
He'd stage the greatest show on earth for her.
Without a net he'd fly from a trapeze,
brave hoops of fire, ride naked through the flames.
She was his circus's still centre. Fifty years
later, seeing those unruly city names:

Blygezight, Prashad Nagar, Lamaha, Laluni street,
he'd still see her, their names again answering her name
until the city's circus, tamed, became Joanstown....

He loved her for the woman she already was.
She loved him for the man he would become.

4. Water Street

If you rode west to the end of Barrack Street
turned left by the power station, passed the koker
and lifted your bicycle over the railway tracks
you'd be where Water Street really began,
running alongside the river like a creek.
Under an old flambouyante, mysterious as porkknockers, poker-
faced fishermen slapped down cards. One, stoned by the heat,
slept in the shadow of the tree's wide overhang,
red petals fallen on the tarred rope of his body, like blood.
The Demerara slid its tongue under the abattoir
where cruising sharks at slaughter time waited for
handouts, like beggars at the Rice Marketing Board.

(Once, when that mud-brown river was in flood,
an alligator was found stranded in the road.
The shops stacked up their bargains like sandbags
as water rose, cresting the doors of mainstream stores :
Bookers, Weiting & Richter, Fogarty's, Sandbach
Parker)
The street, narrowing between two banks, began to match
its rough beginning. Pedalling up Water street
between Barclay's D.C. and O. and the Royal, was like paddling
a canoe up the Demerara (Arawak for 'rough water')
riding the waves of dray carts and donkey carts for the last quarter
mile to the one-way stretch past Bettancourts where the river lay wallowing
under the greenheart boards of the stelling swallowing
fruitsellers' garbage and discarded boxwood crates
until night banged shut the iron Stabroek market gates.

Booker McConnel & Company had towered over the place
until the Great Fire of '46 levelled them

singeing the monarchy of race, eventually darkening the face
of banks and boardrooms, Legislative Council, P.M.
Some names are new: Muneshwer's, Guyana Stores.
The street's the same except for pavement hucksters, cambios,
the raucous now hawking among the destitute.
Beggars patient as driftwood, disposable as plastic bags,
washing their sex in gutters, naked, mute:
derelicts on parade bearing their poverty like flags.
A prodigal would recognize the place at once.
Same old trinity of wealth: Merchant, Middleman, Ponce.
Outnumbered by banks, the Museum still held neutral ground.
He decided to paddle over, go in and look around.

5. The Museum

Same stairway leading to the Natural World
upstairs: the Interior. Same bearded howler
monkey, mouth an oval 0, hand outstretched,
hunched over the visitors' box: "I humbly beg a boon."
Bug-eyed, big-bellied ancestor, a red buffoon
gone at the seams where the stitches had burst letting
the stuffing show, red fur now an oily brown.
There was a painted model, under glass, of the town
made by one of the old curators, complete with trees.
Wood and paper like the one that had burned down.
He stooped to look, his head a giant's. Gulliver
stooping to Lilliput, their river up to his knees.
Beyond the Street the great Cathedral, then the town.
At night the frail, finicky homes with their fretworked Demerara
windows, lit from inside, glowed like magic lanterns
in Joanstown. His giant's eyes dwarfed the avenues running
between the aisles of samaan trees, the shuttered houses,
lit from inside, watching a young couple walk
to her home in silence after an evening spent at the cinema
holding hands during the Disney movie sharing sandwiches
he'd made for her passing the Promenade Gardens
by the Anglican church its bell tolling midnight
like Cinderella's warning bell. They were in love.
This was no fairytale. Their love would live forever
in their hearts. People would say, in years to come,
they were the perfect couple. Nothing could ever part
those two. Only the wedding would be fairytale, they knew.

6. Kingston Methodist

Stone steps ascending to the high, arched, pillared
doorway. Sash windows almost too heavy to open,
(they had to be closed again each time it rained)
mahogany pulpit and pews, two stained
glass windows in the front which caught the sun
in the late afternoon: a pipe organ in the loft
above the pulpit fed by a bellows hand-pumped
by blind Jacob, to the glory of a God he and aunt Winnie
the organist worshipped with music. The galvanized zinc roof
rang in heavy rain. Inside, the church was dark
in daytime: a Methodist version of the Ark.
When rain abruptly concluded the sermon 'Miss Mac' pulled out
all the stops and played an organ Voluntary.
Afterwards, bright eyes twinkling, she would say:
"A pity. We lost some of the Reverend's sermon today."
We knew she had completed the sermon in her own way.
He would become a Methodist. With cousins (the Taitts) he'd call,
(Taitt and McDavid were related, the Woodbine bunch)
play table tennis, go for a swim on the seawall.
One rainy Sunday afternoon, she asked him to stay for lunch.
Aunt and grandmother had agreed that he could stay.
At lunch her eyes said all she was too shy to say.
He knew that they would marry in that church one day.
(But termites were already in the wood; the church's
methodical bats unloaded guano overhead.
After their wedding there, the ceiling gave a lurch
one night and suddenly imploded. No one heard it drop.
Next morning they found a pile of compost with the roof on top).
Their wedding drew a crowd. It was Fairytale
Wedding of the Year : the wedding of Joanstown.
The pews were dressed like bridesmaids with bouquets.

Blind Jacob primed the bellows: aunt Win began
to play. As he sat there on this Day of Days
with the friend who'd stand by him, his Best Man,
he felt intoxicated with joy. What could
be better than this? His body left the polished wood
and floated towards the organ loft. He was hovering above
the choir when they began to sing 'O perfect love…'
She entered through the sunlit doorway, the stained glass
windows burning gold, turquoise, orange, red.
Her dress caught in the late afternoon sun as her father led
her down the flame-embroidered aisle, his face glowing,
lit from inside, his hair aflame, a halo growing
around her hair's corona of fire. He floated down,
taking his place beside her, dumbstruck by the love
that held him there. This then was the best. No harm
could touch them now. Love had made their lives secure.
One photograph shows them standing, married, arm in arm
(his eyes are closed against the flash) at the church door.

EPILOGUE

Ascending the stone steps to his lonely apartment
with its workstation between cold bed and bath
he thought of how he used to mock the sentimental
past, make light of history: old men's feverish
love of faded things, nostalgia, memento mori.
Nearing sixty now he needed his nostalgia fix
each day. His manuscripts and papers stacked upon
their mortuary pinewood shelves already had
that dead, archival look. They were to be a book,
but that was history. He slid a drawer out
on slick metal grooves. Bundles of inked letters
in their dusty cerements, postmarked from a distant land :
his with their oblique, practiced italic slant,
hers written quickly with a musical, impatient hand.
Those letters, faded now, the paper yellowing, freckled
like old onion skin, held all the life he'd lived:
the town, the wife he'd loved. When would the rest of life begin?
And though each time it hurt like knives to look
he'd thrown nothing away. *There* was his book.
Whatever the first half of life might be,
The second half, he knew, would start with memory.

One day he opened his e-mail and downloaded a photograph
his son had found in an old album: idyllic,
taken two years after their marriage. The top half
was the portrait a friend had done of her in acryllic.
The young couple are posing underneath:
not awkwardly, like newlyweds, self-conscious
in their role. Their happiness is as real as grief.
She stands, her arms around him from behind,
fingers clasped together on his chest.

She is smiling. Her whole face glows
with pleasure. Seated, arms almost akimbo,
he is smiling too. His head is turned
slightly, resting on her arm. Again,
his eyes are closed as if he knows that he
will never be this happy ever again.

He'd kept that portrait in a safe, forgotten
place since their first move. In all the moving,
the living in different countries, the constant travelling,
he'd always packed it carefully in its box.
The portrait was commissioned work, a marriage
gift. Now the box was damaged, label gone,
her name inked with a marker pen
across the top.
He opened up the box.
Her eyes kept looking at him as he took the painting out.
They seemed grey in the room's light, without
those green depths he once knew, as though the dark
in the box had drawn the colour out. Something
else was there: a scrapbook he'd forgotten about.
Thumbing through, he found some old, unfinished
poems, a sketch or two, some sepia photographs
including an early one of her he thought he'd lost.
She is seated, smiling, back upright, on the bench
at Barrack Street. The light around her head, her windblown
hair, is a bright halo. Her dress, a simple cotton print,
seems lit from inside: in her arms a small, white dog.
He picked up a poem, now faded to an aquatint,
and wiping away the fog that had settled on his fish-eye lens,
he read:

"They met. It was foretold.
From that moment their love would unfold.
Nothing was clearer.

In love, they first grew bold
to share those secrets they had never told.
Love is a sharer.

In love, he brought gifts old
and rare, but she gave him a heart of gold;
a gift far rarer.

In love, they would withhold
nothing. They'd let their lives be love-controlled.
What could be fairer?

In love, when nights were cold,
they'd let the children share their bed, enfold
them, hold them nearer.

In love they will grow old
together as a pair of shoes grows old
used by one wearer."

WOODBINE
(for Clairmonte)

In those slow-burning days
quietude held passion.
Flambouyantes brooding in heat
hung out red parasols, dropping cool shadows
on back and head. Sunlight splin-
tered East Street canal. We lay
silent, sun-struck, pin hooks baited with bread,
angling for sunfish.
A lizard noosed in grass threshing itself to death
was common play.
Boys will be boys.

But there was that insistent thing
in our flesh that tore
when we ran in the night
dizzy with freedom. It made us gorge
green mangoes, starapples, sweet bursting sapodillas,
taught us to store pleasure
without thought of price.
At Mrs. Cash-
tinheiro's we mixed mauby with 'compress',
dark syrup marbling the ice.
Remember Mary bruk-iron, legendary whore,
empress of vice?
Where now is Lengery, that towering skeleton
we used to jeer?
And there was plump and married Oona who
gave Big John his first sweet taste, I think,
of sin, to our vicarious delight
and fear.

Innocence, always precarious in those days,
vanished that night.

Children at play,
we pulled life by the root
every new day.
Old Baije, mute, vengeful neighbour
could scare us away
from the great tamarind tree,
but not from knowledge of its sweet
and sour fruit.

SWIMMER

Everything he did came easily.
Trees dropped their fruit
for him to catch,
fires lit for him
with one damp match.
Rain filled his bucket to the brim.
The yard, the circles
of cousins, friends,
the childhood games,
the gabled house,
familiar as its housemaids' names
bouyed his young life
so he could swim.

In those green days
boyhood meandered
like a creek
finding its course
changing its mind.
He wanted to leave the source behind,
go where the sun's glow lit the river's rim
making the forest cyclorama dim
to gold.
He longed to sing with tongues of gauldings
blown, like white confetti, across
the river's scrim.
He yearned to skim that changing surface,
smooth as sapodilla skin
or dimpled as a dinner-gong.
Older swimmers said 'Boy, you too young.
That water deep. The currents-them too strong.'

So life went on, the river pursued its course
until one day, years later, it called to him.
He heard its song.
Its voice was hoarse,
raucous as sin.
Its amber face reflected his as he slipped in,
his body a bateau unzipping the dark water's skin.

Later, half-drowned, glug-glugging on a Coke,
sucking a cigarette,
he'd watched as his struck match ignited the dusk
exploding, with a flash of scarlet ibises, into sunset.
Towelled and dry,
his skin smelt of the river's musk.
Swimmer, he knew that smell would stay
for good, like a dark, carcinogenic stain.
Nothing in life would come easy again.

RAINFOREST GUIDE

Walk softly.
Keep your voice down.
Listen to the forest's voice.
Try not to think of ways
you could develop this place.
Yes. There's gold
and we still use it
to make ornaments, sacred jewellery,
things like that.
Sweat of the sun
and so much blood spilled for it.
Yes, diamonds too: and after rain
The silver streams of waterfalls.
Tears of the moon.
How come we're not rich?
Maybe we are.
But not the way you think.
Enjoy what nature has to show.
Try not to think.
But take care.
The beauty of this place
is pitiless. A cut liana
can give water
or corrosive slime.
Fear snakes.
Especially those
dark serpents
in your own mind.
I'm not criticising you.
We all have to understand
our motives. Otherwise
I'd just say piss off, Pizarro

and that would be that.
Right? O.K.
Watch where you walk. Snakes strike
when you're careless.
So why did you come?
Was it to prove
that you were fearless,
you could face danger and live?
Or did you, in the middle of your life,
enter this green depth
for something more than surfaces can give?
This is where deep forest starts.
It will get deeper,
dangerous underfoot. No pathway.
Follow me close.
Walk softly. Keep your voice down.
Pray.

PALACE OF THE PEACOCK
(for Wilson Harris)

A woodskin, mourning its drowned reflection in the mirror
of a creek, scissors the water's black silk.
The steersman, holes for eyes, an old storyteller,
dips the nib of his paddle in the water's ink
and writes : "It was the third day/ of their journey/ from Mariella."
With drowned eyes his twin reads the slick
of his brother's metre, paddling to keep the rhyme.
An ancient Arawak woman in a threadbare shawl
sleeps between them. Her hair will become a waterfall,
her wrinkled skin an escarpment they must climb
falling to a second death to complete the tale.
They will rise with their drowned crew at the bone flute's call
for the wedding of rainbow, mist and granite wall
in the peacock colours of the waterfall's bridal veil.

LESSON FOR TODAY
(for A. J. Seymour)

Nibbling this coffee-soaked nipple
of island bread,
sweeter than madeleines,
sun's in my blood, my head,
and I at a communion service,
sun warming the windowpanes
as the congregation rises slowly for the hymn
'...Lord of the living and the dead...'
Young Irish minister, pink face aflame,
black sleeves rolled up, dog-collar put away,
introduces the well-known, brown guest
who'll read the lesson for today.

Gently-featured, gentle-voiced. The eyes
behind the tortoise-shell-frame glasses
are kind, amused, mildly ironic, gay.
('... and how are you?' he asked afterwards,
laugh-lines crinkling the edges of his smile)

I'd met him once before
at a Sunday symposium. That morning,
poet ruminant, he'd spoken about literature
as a 'communion of minds' with a heady,
hypnotic warmth, like wine, we the communicants.
His words, falling softly, dissolved
like wafers in the mind.
What was it he'd said ?
('Take, eat this bread. This is my body...')

The reading starts. My body seems to melt.
'Now, Makonaima the Great Spirit dwelt...'

JONESTOWN
(for Ian McDonald)

It stained the rivers red. Stir any creek, the red stain shows.
The vowels are howler monkeys roaring, shocked again
by carnage in Paradise, their mouths widening to oval 0's.
Believers felled like lumber for some dumb, millennial plan:
again, spectacular failure of Upright Man.
The site's been cleared. Deceivers and deceived are gone.
Of all that sin-converted host only their sins remain
washed in the unconverted forest's cleansing rain.

SON OF GUYANA
(for Henry Muttoo)

Doan' tell me 'bout Guyana.
I barn deh in t'irty-t'ree.
Meh great-granfadduh was a black man,
granmuddah was a Puttagee.
One ah meh granfadduh was a coolie-man,
ah draw Buck, white an' Chinee.
Dey call it 'the land of six peoples'
but is seven, unless you doan count me.
We had timber, bauxite, diamond an' gol'.
Sugar was king of de crop.
De Union Jack was pun every flagpole
An' class deh-deh pun class, so, wid de whiteman pun tap.

Doan' tell me 'bout Guyana.
I was a small-boy in farty-eight
when black police shoot dung coolie
in de strike at Enmore estate.
Bot' coolie and nigga was me mattie,
but I din't tek it too hard.
Me faddah had a jab in a office
nat in no estate yard.
Hear me:
Class deh-deh pun class, suh, wid de whiteman pun tap.

Doan' tell me about Guyana.
Doan' talk 'bout ole B. G.
Dey call it 'Bookers Guyana'
since was Bookers own all ah we.
Estate, grocery, dry goods, drugstore,
even de boats-dem in de sea!

One year a hell of a fire
burn down dey biggest shap.
Dey lass piece of dey empire,
but you t'ink dat coulda shake t'ings up?
Nah!
Class deh pun class, suh, wid de rich man pun tap

Doan' tell me 'bout Guyana!
I deh-deh in fifty-t'ree.
Cheddie an' Forbes win de elections
and we start fuh feel like we free.
Man! Bookers an' dem start fuh trimble;
dey feel dey gine pass fuh grass!
Class start shiftin' pun class, so, wid de rich man shakin' pun tap.

Doan' tell me 'bout Guyana.
Constitution papah din' dry yet
when de tanks roll down Water Street
like was some damn movie set.
De Black Watch soldiers come
wid dey big black boot an' dey gun
an' dey suntan ile
an' dey skin fulla bile
fuh put class back pun class, suh, wid de rich man pun tap.

Doan' tell me 'bout Guyana.
Nex' elections 'appanjat!' was de shout.
I deh-deh in fifty-seven:
Cheddie win wit'out a doubt.
De rich man start prayin' to heaven
an' de CIA start dey campaign.
Soon dey had we killin' each adduh:
was coolie an' nigga again
while class still deh pun class, suh, wid de rich man pun tap.

Doan' mek joke 'bout Guyana
if you doan' want a cuff in you mout'!
I din' want to leave, you know,
ah jus' feel ah had to get out.
Ah *hads* was to leff Guyana.
Ah leff deh in sixty-one.
Independence was a word pun a banner
an I din' Black nor Indian.
Ah start feelin de strain
a kinda middle-man pain
when class begin mashin' up class, suh, wid de party pun tap.

So doan' tell me 'bout Guyana.
Ah jus' doan' want to hear.
Doan tell me how t'ings deh suh bad now,
every man jack livin' in fear:
how dey usin' dey head
Jus' to ketch a lil' bread
an' how class like it jus' disappear.
I am a son of Guyana, the land that I love so dear,
and ah swear – to meh Gaad ! – ah gine back deh,
but chief ah cyan mek' it dis year.

PROSPERO'S ISLAND
(for Mark)

1. Ferdinand

Shipwrecked,
following the arrows
of a sandpiper's track
on foot, prince
Ferdinand, cosmic cartographer,
checking the beach
for footprints,
screws the island
to his telescopic eye,
sets down his gyroscope.
Stretching the taut ropes
of his back
he reads the dial of the sun.
Sudden rain puckers the sand
marking in braille
this reading down:

'to make a sea-change
you must seek below the surface.
You must drown.'

Righting the spinning earth
he stumbles on,
watching worlds collide
in his mind's cyclotron.

2. Miranda

There, on the beach,
caught by the sun's flash-bulb under azure skies,
mahogany-skinned, her smile like surf
breaking beneath sea-almond eyes,
she might have been the girl on the brochure
of this green, paradisal island.
But mind, her mind has mountains where
deep forests grow, liana-hung:
Another Eden where, as yet
no bird has sung.

It calls to her in dreams.
She cannot go there yet.
There's too much needing to be done
there, on the beach :
each day sand to be swept,
firewood to fetch.
The island's not the paradise it seems.

Lately, there have been storms
and hammering seas
and she must run to comfort Caliban
when he screams.

HAMLET, PRINCE OF DARKNESS

By night
In this enchanted wood,
a jewelled toad comes down to drink
its own reflection
in the stream.
Bubbled eyes, tender as love, reflect
the curvature of earth,
the moon's bright beam.
It's squat, humped body settles on a rock
to dream.

By day
the wattled toad becomes
a thing of dread.
Its slimy back and mottled head
are odious, obscene.
The princess hurries from her bed
to rouse the sleeping queen.

"Alas! To know what I know!
To see what I have seen!"

FAMILY PORTRAIT
(for Mark and Barbara)

The Man is holding a baby in his arms,
his face a lamp, glowing.
The light in his eyes
is the same as the light in his child's bright looking.
His fingers are touching the soft neck, delicately,
as delicately as they will touch a keyboard
to proclaim this forever miraculous borning.
The Woman is resting now. Miracles are hard work.
Their love embraces her. Her love
flows over them, a river over rock.
They are centred now, love-lines secured.
Circling this child, its centre now, their love
will take on wind and rain and all the rest and still
be rock.
This child is blessèd and will bless.

1. LATE SONNET

I've written this late sonnet to say something
my shaky voice could never say to you.
But for poets past middle age, nothing
comes harder, believe me, than hunting new
metaphors. Might as well try forging
steel without the fire to make it true.
And now it's trapped on paper, this awkward thing,
even the sentiment seems paper too;
the poem a dumb creature in its cage
unable to speak as I had meant it to.
If you could free this poem from its page
you'd understand my futile ague then:
that old malarial ache, that ancient rage
that makes old men of poets, poets of old men.

2. CARPE DIEM

When I was young (as old men say) and bold,
I laughed aloud when older heads cried "carpe
diem: seize the day!" The days were mine to hold.
Now, scarred by the beak of Time, that harpy,
I find each day's a load that I must bear
alone; an ageing Atlas still down on one knee,
shoulders and arms aching with that great sphere:
the sheer, astonishing dead weight of me.
They'll say: "Married too young. Was bound to wear
his talents out with husbanding so soon."
A lie, however comforting to hear.
I gave my heart away one afternoon
when I was young and there was time to play.
Now Time has whittled all my love away.

3. OLD MEN SHOULD WRITE

Old men should write, not the young in their prime:
their past's too shallow to enfranchise them.
Just so they write of lasting things, not whine
about love's fleeting, red-rose-bordered hem.
Poets have sung of love since Homer's time
and women have been pleased to find their name
immortalised in some fond poet's rhyme.
But old men should write poetry that strikes like truth,
splitting the heart in two, searing the page,
leaving an ache worse than a raging tooth.
Let them write verse that thunders, lines that rage
at having served the sentences of innocent youth
only to be set free by crooked age,
learning, too late, life's great Untruth.

4. SAINT LUCY

Her name rings, with three long strokes,
the Benedictine convent's angelus.
Lampions are lit. The Vigie lighthouse turns, spokes
of light encircle the blind eyes of Saint Lucy. Benedictus.
The kneeling convent turns its head to that light
like a girl, lips parted, tongue trembling for the Host,
for the sweet, resinous wine of violons, as night
awakens the island's music. It comes up ghost-
like on the Morne: the kla-kla's song, the toutwelle's grieving,
the sad bellow of a lost cruiseliner, leaving,
and I, an old man falling in love again.
That circling light, bright beyond believing,
returns. My words fly like moths to its flame
as the convent's angelus softly rehearses her name.

5.   CATHEDRAL, CASTRIES

He had this ringing inside his head, like bells.
Not Beethoven's divine tinnitus: more
like Michael Angel's cricket sawing away
in Vincent's ruined ear. Sunday he visited
the cathedral again. Same glow, same amber
shafts of sunlight cloudy with Cherubim.
Confessed his sin, Despair. That noise in his ear
was Despair's maddening din. He looked at the paintings
on the walls. Sacred graffiti, faith of the poor.
Baskets of flowers and fruit, the head of black
Saint Jerome, tight hair radiating light
like spokes, the bright blues of another black
saint: St. Omer. His ears will ring now
with that rough singing, those bold strokes.

6. LOVE'S REIGN

Some days it rained in spite of sun. Clouds
would gather in a moment to bring light showers or flood.
A storm broke late one night: she cried aloud.
He held her then as gently as he could
safe in the arms of love. When it was done,
that wind and driving rain, they were in love for good.
Railed now to that instinct, their lives would run
as one life on a double track. It would. It would.
You see that old couple in their kitchen?
They're still in love, watching the kettle boil
together, their passion steady as that hissing
steam, shining like a sheet of kitchen foil.
Tonight, watching the rain clouds gather above,
they'll celebrate the glory of the reign of love.

COUBARIL
(for Kai)

Of island-hopping they'd had their fill,
the god Hurucán and his wife, Hewannorra,
so they decided to settle on Morne Coubaril
overlooking the city of Castries, St. Lucia.

It was a windy house with a view of the hills.
He slung a hammock on the verandah
and watched the wind turn, like green windmills,
the fans of the breadfruit and banana.

She slept indoors (as most wives will)
while Hurucán stretched out on the verandah.
His snoring rumbled and roared until
the island shook with gales and thunder.

Next day there was island-wide hurricane drill.
(Souffriére had experienced torrential rain, and a
river of mud had slid down from a hill)
There was fear in the heart of every islander.

Now, across the sea, on a distant hill
was his cousin Volucan's massive ajoupa
the volcano, Pelée. Martinique was still
nervous, remembering St. Pierre. No wonder

they feared Volucan. In anger he could kill
without warning: life would end with a bang, not a whimper
if Pelée should blow up again. The spill
of the fiery lava of Volucan's temper

had frightened the Lucians, who, after that thrill,
told themselves that if Hurucán's snores could make thunder,
his shouts might send hurricanes from Coubaril.
A delegation was formed, thirteen in number,

to suggest that he leave. Hurucán sat quite still
when the councillors came, introducing commander-
in-chief, Alcindor, whose voice sounded shrill
when he spoke to the god asking him to surrender

his unwelcome tenancy on Morne Coubaril.
Hurucán smiled. His face showed no anger.
He rested huge arms on the verandah grille.
"This sounds like my wild cousin Volucan's slander.

Were you to invite me to show you *my* skill
I could shatter your houses like just so much tinder.
The country could never afford to rebuild.
I'd drown all your fields with rain, lightning and thunder.

I have come here in peace and not with ill-will
to retire. I've no wish to cause any terror.
I used to sleep indoors, but that was until
my snoring began to disturb Hewannorra."

Everyone listened, then grew very still.
It seemed they had made a terrible blunder.
There were fields to be planted and quotas to fill.
It could hurt them if *one* of their farms should go under.

The thought of this faux pas was making them ill:
they had risked stirring up the god Hurucán's anger.
The silence that followed was awkward to fill.
Then a voice called "Hurucán!"from the back of the verandah.

It was Dujon, seated on a window sill
listening to the conference on the verandah.
He jumped down and walked to the front until
he was standing alongside Alcindor, the Commander.

Dujon wiped his face, using his shirt as a towel.
"Bo'jou' to you and your spouse, Hewannorra,
messiay. Now, to expedite this impasse without quarrel,
I suggess *you* sleep inside and *she* on verandah.

then our crops they don't die and the rivers don't spill
because of your terrible snoring like thunder."
Hurucán looked like he'd swallowed a camel.
His eyes opened wide and got rounder and rounder

until everyone felt that their lives were in peril.
Then the god laughed. The wind tore asunder
a field of bananas as it roared downhill:
the ships in the harbour started to founder.

It rattled the roofs on Morne Coubaril.
"My friend, he said sputtering, your idea is better
than the solution suggested by your city council.
Wait here (then he smiled), I will find Hewannorra.

I don't want to shout – think of those I might kill! –
I'll seek the advice of my dear wife and partner."
He looked at Dujon, then he looked at the council.
Then, stifling his laughter, he left the verandah.

A decision was made. From November to April
Hurucán would sleep indoors. From May to October
he'd sleep on the verandah with his back to the grille.
The councillors thanked him. The crisis was over.

There's a National Trust plaque on Morne Coubaril
honouring Hurucán and his wife Hewannorra;
and, to this very day, island hurricane drill
begins in May and ends in October.

THE HOOK

Our silver, fish-bellied aircraft takes off
tilting the island, its white roofs slanting dangerously,
until finally even the sea's blue slides away
slow-fading from cerulean blue to grey.
Munching a Bermuda chicken sandwich I peer
through the scratched plexiglass and feel, with a start,
as the clouds clear,
the tug of that island's hook in my heart.

Breathing in that cold, thin air I'm pinned
squirming in my seat, out of my element,
back arched like the small bream young Sacha
dangled, wide-eyed, from the hook of an angler's line
baited with meat from a Bermuda chicken sandwich.

And though I should know that 'nothing gold can stay'
I want to remember forever that magical cay
where a boy's smile sparkled like the bright hull
of a boat with small fry leaping in its wake
like a handful of pebbles thrown or like white beads
of ocean spray, or like the flash of the fish he let go
to swim its way through the sun-sprinkled, glittering water
of that beautiful bay.

TUTORIAL
(for Tom Andrews)

Writing, his heart's all rock.
Hunting, his mind's all teeth.

Once, out fishing with him
(Japanese style, he said)
I watched his poet's eye, blue as the sea,
line up that tower of learning on Cave hill
with his boat's nodding prow.
Seasick, my stomach heaved
when I saw how
those poet fingers could clench hard
to tear the red leaves
of a Barracuda's gills
with the same, dark, feral joy
as write a poem.

"Listen.
On this deep blue unsteady sea
no one needs books.
All speech is spare.
Leave eloquence and literary frills
to sterile academic minds grinding
their sterile academic mills.
Words are mere bait.
Nibs are the baited hooks for grappling life."

A bite !
The reel unwinds, taut as a sentence; and now
another poem surfaces, leaping on its hook
and flashing silver
like a knife.

ZODIAC DANCE
(for Ivan)

His element was air, his humour melancholy.
Born Scorpio in Saturn, he could not bear the folly
of a commonplace romance.
A sudden blow: O brightening glance!
In a flash he saw that love, to defy the Fates
or herald a new dawn
would have to boldly go where love had never gone.
Taking his cue from the great master, Yeats,
he'd cast his lover as a Leda lost
in feathered blizzards of the Swan.
Winged Jupiter descending, he'd overpower
her ignorant body and mind, enhance
her Spartan love with arcane knowledge, shower
constellations down to make the zodiac dance.

A Capricorn much younger than her years,
goat-born, with the goat's nervous, sidelong glance,
horned by timidity and secret fears
she yawned at the full moon's radiance.
Her element was water: every dawn she drowned in sleep.
Horoscope-haunted ('an old aquaintance calls.
You break a promise you had sworn to keep.')
She longed to give her body to the dance;
but to his mystical music dancing
was difficult for her, and wrong.
the melody was strange, metaphysical:
his music roused her mind, flung her headlong.
She clung to surer footholds, goatskin drumming
to the steady clamour of a gong.
No soaring melodies for her. No song.

In his terrible, vague fluttering of wings
unutterable things were left to chance.
How could she tell the dancer from the dance?

When, finally, he made the music stop,
she had put on none of his knowledge or power.
It was with great relief
he let her drop.

CURTAIN CALL
(for Wilbert Holder)

Dead?

That fine, that skillful
actor-man, that
Midnight Robber, dead?
Jesus, we'll miss him.

And yet I think we lost him
long ago.
Since boys we saw him go
that road of make-believe,
acting whatever came into his head.
So many skins put on
so many shed.
The show was all.
Real life could wait.
His art was all the life he led.
To get inside a part and play it well,
so well that he became the thing
he played, losing himself.
Yes, he was good: One of the best we had.
We all applauded what he played,
it was so real.
But when you got inside his head
he would be somewhere else instead.

Up there, I bet he's taking
curtain calls again, getting applause,
knocking them dead.

POSEIDON

Old Pa sits
In his bentwood chair.
Smoke from his pipe curls slowly up
In the room's still air.
He looks at the world
From his eye's grey rim.

And the world without
And the world within

Have little to do with the likes of him.

And the way we live
And the way we die

Mean nothing at all to his jaundiced eye.

But as he breathes out
But as he breathes in

Whole horizons seem to swim
In his watery eye.

LITTORAL

Alone
on Worthing beach
watching the waves teach patience
to the coral's tongue,
learning from those young
sea-urchins to sit still, my head a stone,
I let the sandflies worry my sun-stroked eyes,
my driftwood legs
and listen to the waves rehearsing the futility
of flesh and bone.
Perhaps today my life, repetitive as the indifferent wave,
will break, losing its hurts
to yield a pattern
like the sea-egg's intricately patterned shell.
Perhaps all will be well.

Sun burns this lesson on my back:

"Do not expect the line
that hooks you in
ever to grow slack,
nor every tugging root
reveal its cause.
Body must break
put on that rack."

A wave breaks and recedes.
The pebbles clatter.
Like applause.

MORNE FORTUNE

No man's an island (he'd read John Donne). His creative urge
sailed where the collective imagination sent.
He'd be like Harris's Dreamer, charting rivers of a continent
with a drowned crew, feeling that Atlantic surge.
When, upriver, his poetic craft got stuck
(that mud sucked men and poems down without a trace)
he figured island life might change his luck :
he'd seek the Antillean Genius of Place.

He managed to get a creative writer's grant
to live in Lucian hills, find a new slant.
"Bon bagai ! My island *steep* in poetry, boy !"
encouraged a poet friend, St. Lucian born.
In Castries, boarding a mini-van, a sudden rush of joy.
The bearded driver was Triton, blowing his wreathèd horn!
That sloe-eyed woman, Greek there, a black Helen of Troy !
The humped hills, shouldering stars above the Morne
thrilled and intimidated him, like Wordsworth's Boy.
That nightride up Morne Fortune left him numb.
His continental brain, like a container lorry
grinding gears, changed into first.
At this height would his poems come
and stay until he'd winged them so they could glide down?
Tomorrow, at dusk, his poem-time, he'd know the worst.

From his high verandah dawn woke commonplace,
transparent as a housewife in her shift.
Trees in curlers, ravine breaking wind,
the hills still in their white mosquito nets of mist,
the valley smoking an early cigarette.
A light rain falling: the Morne washing its face.

It would take genius to make such flimsy stuff
reflect the Antillean Genius of Place.
The island, twinned by laureate poetry to Greece,
still wasn't Greek: the Cathedral chimes mimicked Big Ben.
No city sign said "Ithaca/Castries".
But if not Lucian landscape, well what then?
At sundown, when he launched a trial poem,
the thing glided across the town and fell into the sea.
He was old Daedalus watching his son drown.

One day, in town, hoping to find a poem or two
that he'd sent down, he stopped in for a beer
and stayed to listen to some poetry at the Rose & Crown.
The place was full of poets, one waxing eloquent
sipping a Piton (he'd sworn off Bounty for Lent),
swivelling his grey, unfocussed lion's eyes:

"You-all sit up there on your Pegasses;
You waiting in case fame or fortune calls?
Genius is jus' a man wif' talent and
a bold attitude. You watch my smoke, gasson.
I take life by the balls, you know?, keep poetry
in my grip (O.K. big joke. I don't mean a suitcase.)
Look. The Muse is a Jablesse, as you know well.
You have to take she so (grabbing the bottle)
and buss she mouf' until you taste success.
You can't play noble and win a Nobel.
Gasson you have to capay diem if you want
to write at all. Get off your high horse man.
You know? Pride goeth before a fall."

That sundown, back on Morne Fortune, he cried
to be unhorsed, envisioned, blinded, like Saul,
like Walcott, even like V.S. Naipaul.

MUDHEAD, PAINTER

Begin with a dark grey wash on this sky's canvas.
Before it dries touch the belly of that cloud
with a wet brush tipped with black, then paint the deluge.
Let the paint flow in rivers like Orinocco
or Amazon discolouring an ocean to make beaches
of mud, not sand. Add a dewlapped lizard
drinking from the green teflon bowl of a lilly's
dinnerplate leaves, rain forming quicksilver necklaces
which break letting the bright pearls fall to make the lotuses
nod approval as the trench fills up with paint
the colour of mud. Paint a farmer, Indian
or African, shirtless, up to his calves in mud
labouring towards a bawling, mud-coloured cow
tied to a stake. Fur with green mold the wooden
stilts of his crude house. Paint a hammock,
rice-bag or sugar-bag, under the house between
two stilts. Let the house stand marooned in water,
galvanize roof pouring. Pictorial, not picturesque.
(after the rain it will contemplate its own
limpid reflection). Paint small black and brown
boys naked in the rain, tins scooping
water up to throw in a muddy Phagwa
game, innocent and raceless as the genip-seed
buds of their childish penises. Name the painting
"Buxton /Friendship." Sign it "Mudhead, Guyana".
Date it nineteen sixty-one, the year you left.

NEW POETRY TITLES

BETWEEN THE FENCE AND THE FOREST
JENNIFER RAHIM

Comparing herself to a douen, a mythical being from the Trinidadian forests whose head and feet face in different directions, Jennifer Rahim's poems explore states of uncertainty both as sources of discomfort and of creative possibility. The poems explore a Trinidad finely balanced between the forces of rapid urbanisation and the constantly encroaching green chaos of tropical bush, whose people, as the descendants of slaves and indentured labourers, are acutely resistant to any threat to clip their wings and fence them in, whose turbulence regularly threatens a fragile social order. In her own life, Rahim explores the contrary urges to a neat security and to an unfettered sense of freedom and her attraction to the forest 'where tallness is not the neighbour's fences/ and bigness is not the swollen houses/ that swallow us all'. It is, though, a place where the bushplanter 'seeing me grow branches/ draws out his cutting steel and slashes my feet/ since girls can never become trees'.

Jennifer Rahim was born and grew up in Trinidad. Her first collection of poems, *Mothers Are Not the Only Linguists* was published in 1992. She also writes short fiction and criticism. She currently lectures in English at the University of West Indies in Jamaica.

SPECIFICATIONS
ISBN: 1-900715-27-9
Price: Stg£7.99 / US$13.60 / CAN$19.20
Pages: 88
Date of Publication: July 2002

HORIZON
STANLEY GREAVES

Stanley Greaves brings a painter's perceptions and musician's ear to the writing of this substantial selection of his poetry written over the past forty years. He describes his painting as 'a kind of allegorical story-telling' and the same kind of connections between the concrete and the metaphysical are found in his poems.

Greaves guesses at a background that includes African, Amerindian and European ancestry, but declines to relate to any of these in an exclusive way. Rather he writes out of a creole sensibility that celebrates Guyanese diversity: Afro-Guyanese folkways, Amerindian legend and Hindu philosophy.

To enter the collection is to discover a whole, self-created world of Blakean richness, one which is never static, but growing to encompass new elements. Greaves' is a dialectical vision, alert both to the movements of history and the minutiae of daily change.

Stanley Greaves was born in Guyana. He studied art in the UK and was head of the Division of Creative Arts at the University of Guyana for several years. He left Guyana in the 1980s and has been resident in Barbados since that time. He is one of the Caribbean's most distinguished artists with major exhibitions in the UK (The Elders, with Brother Everald Brown) and Europe as well as throughout the Caribbean. The collection includes ten line drawings by Stanley Greaves.

SPECIFICATIONS
ISBN: 1-900715-57-0
Price: Stg£9.99 / US$17.00 / CAN$24.00
Pages: 162
Date of Publication: July 2002

Peepal Tree Press publishes a wide selection of outstanding fiction, poetry, drama, history and literary criticism with a focus on the Caribbean, Africa, the South Asian diaspora and Black life in Britain. Peepal Tree is now the largest independent publisher of Caribbean writing in the world. All our books are high quality original paperbacks designed to stand the test of time and repeated readings.

All Peepal Tree books should be available through your local bookseller, though you are most welcome to place orders direct with us. When ordering a book direct from us, simply tell us the title, author, quantity and the address to which the book should be mailed. Please enclose a cheque or money order for the cover price of the book, plus £1 / US$3.20 / CAN$5.50 towards postage and packing.

Peepal Tree sends out regular e-mail information about new books and special offers. We also produce a yearly catalogue which gives current prices in sterling, US and Canadian dollars and full details of all our books. Contact us to join our mailing list.

You can contact Peepal Tree at:

17 King's Avenue
Leeds LS6 1QS
United Kingdom

e-mail hannah@peepal.demon.co.uk
tel: 44 (0)113 245 1703
fax: 44 (0)113 245 9616